Presented to:

_____

By:

_____

Date:

_____

The Golfer's Tee Time Devotional

Inspiration from the Rich Traditions of Golf

The Golfer's Tee Time Devotional

Inspiration from the Rich Traditions of Golf

Tulsa, Oklahoma

2nd Printing

The Golfer's Tee Time Devotional
ISBN 1-56292-008-1
Copyright © 1997 by Honor Books
P.O. Box 55388
Tulsa, Oklahoma 74155

Written by James R. Bolley

"Golf is deceptively simple and endlessly complicated, it satisfies the soul and frustrates the intellect. It is at the same time rewarding and maddening — and it is without a doubt the greatest game mankind has ever invented."

— Arnold Palmer

Contents

Foreword 11

Introduction 15

1 Off the First Tee 19

2 The Importance of Fundamentals 29

3 The Short Game 39

4 Putting 47

5 When Your Game Falls Apart 57

6 Recovery 69

7 Hazards 77

8 Good Equipment 87

9 Knowing Your Game 97

10 Managing Your Game 107

11 The Mental Game 117

12 Sportsmanship 125

13 Etiquette 135

14 A Sense of History 143

15 Golf's Great Moments 155

16 To Get Better, Just Play! 163

17 Watching the Pros 171

18 The Course: Perfect World, Treacherous Golf . . 183

19 The Nineteenth Hole: Friendship
   and Fellowship 193

Foreword

Golf. To love the game of golf is to appreciate its character and its challenges. It is a game that requires dedication and daily attention to the basics that can make you either a hack on Saturday afternoon, or the winner of one of the game's treasured "majors."

While I have been out on tour, I realized that the experiences of life are as exhilarating and exciting as the wonderful game of golf. As a Christian, I realize that my gifts and abilities as a professional golfer are directly from God. With that in mind, I know that just as champions rise beyond the mastery of skills and techniques to win in pressure-filled competition, we can also use our gifts and abilities from God to be champions in life.

Being a champion in life is what this book is all about. As it parallels life-changing principles with the rich traditions and history of the game of golf, *The Golfer's Tee Time Devotional* gives you powerful insights and practical information with the flavor and drama of my favorite way to spend a weekend — golf.

This easy-to-read book doesn't preach, but simply gives you an opportunity to be coachable. The insights in this book will help you make the game of golf, and more importantly the game of life, even more enjoyable.

Many times God speaks to us through the things we love to do; sports, hobbies, work, and friendships. As a professional golfer, I am often asked for tips or advice. So here it is — listen to what God can say to you through the great game of golf.

Tom Lehman
1996 British Open Champion
1996 Tour Champion
1996 Vardon Trophy Winner
1996 PGA Player of the Year

"When you reflect on the combination of characteristics that golf demands of those who would presume to play it, it is not surprising that golf has never had a truly great player who was not also a person of extraordinary character."

— Frank D. "Sandy" Tatum, Jr.

Introduction

Looking at the freshly cut fairway of lush green grass from the first tee box, a player thinks about the coming round of golf with friends who will be sharing the next few hours together. On this course, distractions will be set aside, and focus will be centered on the moments at hand. Throughout the round, each shot will be an event in itself, not influenced by past failures or ignored for future successes.

This is as perfect an environment as man can make, with manicured fairways, tall majestic trees, lush shrubs, and beautiful greens. But, every golfer knows there are hazards, out-of-bounds markers, bad lies, and challenging shots waiting all over this beautiful little piece of the world.

As the round begins, everyone is equal. Handicaps have leveled the playing field. Each golfer responds to various challenges, disappointments, and great shots based upon his own temperament. The next few hours will include moments of hopeful imagination, great fellowship, and subtle courtesies which make each participant feel special.

Golf is a fascinating game in which individuals play against each other and the course. Competition gives way to congratulations for a great shot, or encouragement in tough situations. Golf is most enjoyable when played with friends.

Golf is a game in which a ten-year-old can play with an eighty-year-old and still compete favorably. Controlled finesse is more valuable than uncontrolled power. A poor three-foot putt counts as much as a bad two-hundred-fifty-yard drive. Holes are played over hundreds of yards, but success or failure is defined in mere inches.

Golf involves more than the simple mechanics of swinging a club to strike a ball. It is a game of roller-coaster emotions — periods of extreme pressure and moments of pure joy.

This isn't a book about the mechanics of golf; there are hundreds of teaching aids about these subjects. But, this is a book about better golf. It attempts to look at the game from its very nature — the ambiance, the feel, the etiquette, and the history of this most frustrating of activities enjoyed by millions of people every day around the world.

This book is also about our relationship to God. It examines the many aspects of the game of golf as pictures of our spiritual lives as we give ourselves to the greatest of teaching pros, God's own Son, Jesus Christ. Through this devotional, may God speak to you about yourself, His words of instruction and wisdom found in the Bible, and the greatest of all challenges — the Christian life.

Chapter 1

"The odds of hitting a duffed shot increase by the square of the number of people watching."

— Henry Beard

Mulligan's Laws

"One of the most fascinating things about golf is how it reflects the cycle of life. No matter what you shoot — the next day you have to go back to the first tee and begin all over again and make yourself into something."

— Peter Jacobsen

The action at the first tee of a major golf tournament shouldn't be missed by those who come to watch the professionals. Players are introduced to a politely applauding crowd. Past tournament accomplishments are announced, along with the home course and country of origin of each player. Every eye in the crowd is focused on the professional as he addresses the ball. Everyone is completely still as the first shot of the round is immediately followed by a moment of expectant silence and then another round of applause.

Average golfers can only imagine the kind of pressure a large crowd at the first tee creates. Watching the professionals, it is easy to imagine hitting a great shot like the one just witnessed. It is also easy to shudder at the very thought of being in front of the same crowd, hitting a duff which stops a few yards ahead of the tee box.

There is something about the first tee shot which seems to influence the day, the round, the front nine, or at least the first hole. It is the getting started point which sets the focus and confidence for the next few shots. It can be like a runner stumbling out of the blocks with a false start, or a baseball player watching the first hit of the game clear the center field fence.

Whether in front of a crowd with hundreds of people, or three other friends in a foursome, any player can experience "first tee jitters." The expectations golfers put on themselves to perform well, along with the desire to impress other people, can make them overcompensate for weaknesses or just plain break down in the swing.

Those who conquer the "first tee jitters" prepare themselves both physically and mentally. On the practice tee they don't just "hit some." They loosen up, stretch muscles, visualize the shots they want to make, and mentally prepare themselves for the first tee. First tee shots aren't left to chance. They are prepared for and practiced.

"Men of dignity and business acumen when sailing through the corridors of power with a flock of underlings and yes-men in their wake become semi-paralytic when overcome by first tee nerves."

— Ben Wright

⚲ REFLECTIONS

Often times we have trouble getting started with new commitments or changes in our lives. Expectations of other people, fear of the unknown, and lack of confidence give us those "getting started jitters."

Your relationship with God can prepare you for those moments when you must step up to a challenge and face it head-on.

Overcoming apprehension doesn't just happen. It starts with a life that is transformed by a personal experience with God. Strength to begin again, or to just keep going in the face of adversity, comes from a heart that knows that God is the true Source of courage.

⛳ PRAYER

Lord, prepare me for the new experiences of my life by giving me confidence in You.

Replace fear with an assured faith. Motivate me to step up when the time is right, and boldly express what You have done in my life.

If I never stand before thousands of people, prepare me for that one person whose life can be changed by my expression of Your love and grace.

Give me courage when the pressure is on, and confidence when so much is at stake.

⛳ SCRIPTURE

"Be strong and of good courage; do not be afraid,
nor be dismayed, for the lord your God is with
you wherever you go."

Joshua 1:9 NKJV

Chapter 2

The Importance of Fundamentals

> *"I probably have forgotten more about golf than I have ever learned."*
>
> — Jack Nicklaus

"...practice puts...brains in your muscles."
— Sam Snead

All sports have fundamentals. Golf isn't any different in that regard. Fundamentals are the basics of how to effectively play the game. Along with practicing these basic elements, the golfer adds mental concentration and focus.

Fundamentals can be as simple as stance, grip, and swing. Sometimes these basics are complicated with fundamentals of each fundamental. Each element is broken down into smaller elements for analysis and training. The swing becomes: the take away, the downward motion, the point of impact, and the follow through. Components of each fundamental are memorized and practiced so that muscles are tuned to *feel* the correct motions and results.

The fundamentals of golf are best learned from a teaching professional. It is more difficult to break bad habits than to learn correct habits in the first place. Having someone else to watch, teach, and advise can help in the formation of the habits of good golf mechanics.

The best professional golfers in the world receive coaching and practice the fundamentals before each tournament round. They realize that difficult shots are made by simple adjustments in the golf swing.

Whenever their game begins to deteriorate, they know that the best thing to do is return to the basics.

Problems on the golf course are usually caused by a breakdown in fundamentals. The value of good coaching and the eye of a trained professional can help get a game back or move it to the next level.

"I have loved playing the game and practicing it. Whether my schedule for the following day called for a tournament round or merely a trip to the practice tee, the prospect that there was going to be golf in it made me feel privileged and extremely happy. I couldn't wait for the sun to come up so that I could get out on the course again."

— Ben Hogan

REFLECTIONS

Just as there are fundamentals in the game of golf, there are also fundamentals in our spiritual lives.

You may face difficult challenges to your beliefs, but remember, your success in those situations is primarily based upon the fundamentals of your faith and your trust in God.

Sometimes you need the help of others to coach you and help you learn the basics of your faith. Whenever your life begins to deteriorate spiritually, you most likely need to get back to the fundamentals of your walk with God.

Just as we must learn to feel and memorize the basics of a good golf swing, so it is with the fundamentals of our spiritual lives. With the Holy Spirit as your helper, as you purpose to learn and grow by consistently practicing these "fundamentals," you will become more and more confident in your daily walk of faith.

PRAYER

Lord, teach me the fundamentals of my Christian faith. If I have picked up bad habits which keep me from being effective, help me to be receptive to good coaching.

I depend on You to teach me, guide me, and help me to remember the basic principles and power of Your love. I pray that the fundamentals of my faith will be a natural and effortless part of my life and service for You.

SCRIPTURE

This is love: not that we loved God, but that he loved us and sent his Son as an atoning sacrifice for our sins. Dear friends, since God so loved us, we also ought to love one another. No one has ever seen God; but if we love one another, God lives in us and his love is made complete in us.

1 John 4:10-12

Chapter 3

The Short Game

"*The hardest shot is a mashie at ninety yards from the green, where the ball has to be played against an oak tree, bounced back into a sand trap, hits a stone, bounces on the green, and then rolls into the cup. That shot is so difficult I have only made it once.*"

— Zeppo Marx

"Dear God, don't let me chili-dip this. Put it in the bunker if you want. Maybe I can hole it from the bunker."

— Chi Chi Rodriquez
on a wedge shot

The shot is from eighty yards out, into the wind, uphill to a small and slopping green which will feed the ball back to the front. The green is protected on both sides by large sand traps. The flag is to the front of the green on the only level portion of the putting surface. The greens are fast and very hard today.

This is when golf is really fun! Everything about this situation requires analysis of some important elements of the short game.

Success requires a combination of skill, control, and finesse.

How should a shot from this distance be played? What club should be selected? What will the wind do to the ball; how far and in what direction will it be moved? Is it best to play to the back of the green and try to spin the ball to the front, or can it be made to land near the flag in the level area? Is this a low soft shot under the wind, or a high spinning shot working with the wind?

Successful golfers have to answer all of these kinds of questions, and more, based upon specific skills and knowledge of what works best for them.

Everyone analyzes such situations a little differently — some a little more, some a little less. Some depend a great deal upon luck, while others make adjustments for every factor in the shot.

The ability to make these adjustments, and become successful at playing the short game in a variety of conditions, adds tremendously to enjoyment of the game.

As golfers begin to realize that chance is playing a less significant role in their success, they begin to take control of their game. The short game is one of the first areas where this change becomes apparent.

When it is no longer a question of "can I get it there?," it becomes more a question of "how effectively can I get it there?"

The concerns which can now be put out of the mind make room for the ideas and challenges that make the game more relaxing and enjoyable.

What *is* the best way to play the short game? Think distance only? Consider where to land the ball on the green, and where it will go after it lands? Hit a low trajectory shot or a high shot? Try to spin the ball back, or keep it low and run it to the cup?

At the practice range, work should be concentrated on shots which can be used in a variety of situations. Practice should not be focused on just hitting the ball, but on taking aim and placing the ball at specific targets, which will develop particular skills and a feel for different shots.

A variety of shot-making skills in the short game can shave strokes off the final score and add a new dimension of enjoyment to each round played.

REFLECTIONS

Many of us have a one-dimensional approach to our relationship with God. We have learned one thing that seems to work, and we try to apply it in every situation. But, our faith in God should be active and alive with a power which leads, directs, and responds to every unique situation we encounter.

Many times we need to take our spiritual lives to the next level. We should strive to reach a level of confidence that is less dependent upon luck and circumstances and is more a reflection of control and purpose.

It is no longer a question of "can I live a godly life?," but more a question of "how can I be the most effective in my life with God?"

We need to become skilled at putting together the gifts and abilities God has given us so that we can face every situation with a faith that is both active and responsive.

PRAYER

Lord, grant me confidence and faith in the gifts and abilities You have given me. Help me to use them effectively for You.

I know that success in my spiritual life does not depend upon me doing great things for You, but upon You doing great things through me.

Add new dimensions to my faith and give me wisdom in every situation.

As I come to know You better, serving You becomes pure joy.

SCRIPTURE

And God is able to make all grace abound to you, so that in all things at all times, having all that you need, you will abound in every good work.

2 Corinthians 9:8

Chapter 4

Putting

"Why am I using a new putter? Because the old one didn't float too well."

— Craig Stadler

"Putting is like wisdom — partly a natural gift and partly the accumulation of experience."

— Arnold Palmer

Golf can really be divided into two separate games. The first game is played in the air. It doesn't matter what drives and iron shots fly over. The ball is not affected by the lay of the land as it soars through the sky, but by the impact of the club at the point of contact and by the wind while it is in flight. Once the ball strikes the earth, it does bounce and roll, but generally this final movement represents only a fraction of the total distance traveled.

The second game is played on the putting surface. Here an entirely different set of conditions must be considered.

Putting has been called both a science and an art. It is a combination of geometry, physics, botany, and psychology. A player can drive straight down the middle, reach the green in regulation, and spin the ball to a perfect stop, then step up and putt himself into utter frustration.

Putting requires an awareness of the total picture: What forces seen and unseen will exert an effect on this stroke? How much break is there? What is the right speed? What is the texture of the grass — is it long or short, thick or thin, wet or dry? What imperfections in the green will affect this putt?

Putting is concerned with "lines" — straight lines and curved lines, uphill lines and downhill lines, slow lines and fast lines. How a golfer reads and interprets these lines makes all the difference between success or failure. This is the science of putting.

Putting is also an art. It involves confidence and feel, the ability to visualize exactly what needs be accomplished and to execute the precise stroke required to reach that goal. The art of putting is the ability to put together all of the pieces consistently and smoothly, making every element work together harmoniously.

Great golfers are great putters. Most of the time, strokes are saved on the putting surface, not in the air. Eagles and birdies are more often made with great putts than with long drives or spectacular iron shots.

REFLECTIONS

Our spiritual life is a multi-faceted experience. The world around us is constantly exerting forces on us which will affect our efforts to live for God.

Similar to putting, we need to be able to "read" these influences and make corrections accordingly.

Just as great golfers are able to adjust successfully to the subtle nuances of the putting surface, so we can depend upon the gentle leading of God — that still small voice, which speaks to our hearts of His corrections and adjustments — to get us lined up with His purpose and perfect will.

With God's help we can be aware of all the spiritual influences in our lives. We can know what is affecting us, what is pulling us one way or the other, what forces externally and internally are keeping us from enjoying an exciting walk with Him.

It could be said that, like putting, faith is partly a supernatural gift and partly the accumulation of experience.

Wherever the "lie," whatever the situation we may face in life, we can trust God. We can know by experience that His love and grace will supply all the confidence and faith we need to walk with Him.

PRAYER

Lord, help me to "read" things right. Give me the confidence that only You can give.

Help me to understand everything that has an impact on my life and to adjust my stroke and aim accordingly.

Help me to see Your purposes clearly and not be satisfied with "just getting it close."

Lord, help me to realize and remember that I usually get the best "read" when I am on my knees.

SCRIPTURE

And this is my prayer: that your love may abound
more and more in knowledge and depth of insight, so
that you may be able to discern what is best and may
be pure and blameless until the day of Christ, filled
with the fruit of righteousness that comes through
Jesus Christ — to the glory and praise of God.

Philippians 1:9-11

Chapter 5

"It took me seventeen years to get three thousand hits in baseball. I did it in one afternoon on the golf course."

— Hank Aaron

"It is the one great democratic quirk of golf. Even the greatest players must occasionally stand by helplessly as their game disintegrates."

— Michael Konik

Sooner or later it happens to every golfer. Whether a weekend duffer or a seasoned professional, every golfer inevitably experiences the frustrations of his game "falling apart." It can last for just one hole or for several holes, for just one round or for several rounds. Whatever its length or severity, the effect mentally and emotionally can be devastating.

One of the oldest stories in golf is about a Scottish golfer who threw his clubs into the sea after a frustratingly poor round, and almost drowned trying to rescue them.

It is this very problem which has spawned the marketing and sales of training videos, swing aids, visualization exercises, and sports psychology.

When things go bad, serious golfers will go to almost any length to bring themselves back. Hours upon hours of hitting practice balls at the driving range — making adjustments in the swing plane, the grip, the take away, the follow through, the elbows, the hands — the changes go on and on.

Most professional golfers claim that when their game falls apart, they don't try to change much of anything. The most frequently heard statement is, "I just try to get back to the basics." If the professional adjusts anything at all, it is usually one or two small elements in his swing or some other area in which he knows he is having problems.

Probably the most common element that must be watched when things begin to go wrong is tempo or speed.

Nick Faldo says, "My swing sometimes gets too forceful. So I soften my arms, trying to swing it slow, to get some tempo to my game. I do that and it feels good."

Maintaining the proper tempo in the golf swing can be a problem because so many things must work together. Something happening too soon or too late can cause the entire shot to be a disaster.

As a game begins to disintegrate, often emotions take over, producing anger and frustration. This emotional upheaval can bring about a change in swing tempo or lead to the forcing of shots.

Great players know how to compose themselves, refocus, and pull their game back together as quickly as possible. They realize that controlling themselves, slowing down, and going back to what they know will work can be the most effective road to recovery.

REFLECTIONS

Any one of us can face a breakdown in our spiritual life.

Like amateur golfers, at the first sign of a problem often we rush to the local bookstore for training tapes, videos, or "expert" advice and information.

At other times, like disgusted duffers who hang up their clubs in the garage and take up another sport, we are tempted to set our spiritual lives aside and try to avoid the frustrations and feelings of failure.

When faced with such trying times, we can learn to put our spiritual lives back together from the same lessons we follow in putting our golf game back on track.

First of all, it is important to get back to the "basics." God's forgiveness and grace can restore the joy of our relationship with Him. Returning to the fundamentals of what God has done for us can re-invigorate our life.

Second, it is helpful to think about tempo or timing. This is similar to the timing or tempo of the golf swing. It is the natural flow of the swing that makes all of the other elements happen at the right time.

The answer is not to try to force the action, but to allow the elements of our spiritual lives to come back together naturally and effectively. Like the professional golfer's swing, we know where the adjustments need to be made, and how to work on the timing of all the little things that make such a difference in the final outcome.

When golfer Corey Pavin was asked about his reaction to lapses in his game, he replied: "I got so caught up in the mechanics that when I hit a bad shot I would wonder what was wrong with my swing, when in actuality there wasn't anything wrong. I just hit a bad shot."

Often we get so caught up with what has gone wrong in our lives that we feel that we just can't go on. We try to analyze what has happened, instead of realizing that it was just a mistake. We can take our faults and shortcomings to God in prayer and then, by faith and trust in His grace, continue our journey with Him.

"I don't really try to change anything. My faults in my swing have always been my legs. I've got long legs, and they kind of get all over the place sometimes. I work on that a little bit in the setup, but nothing serious. Just trying to get back to the basics. So far, it's working."

— Ernie Els quoted in
Sky magazine, March 1996

Prayer

Lord, when things seem to fall apart in my spiritual life, help me to get back to the basics. Help me to overcome the frustrations and anxiety that would drag me down into despair.

Forgive me, and show me how to set the right tempo so that everything works together again. When I make mistakes, help me to recognize them for what they are, admit them, correct them, and find Your forgiveness.

If everything does fall apart, help me not to give into the temptation to "hang it up and quit." Instead, give me that same joy and peace that I felt when I first believed in You.

SCRIPTURE

Create in me a pure heart, O God, and renew a
steadfast spirit within me. Do not cast me from
your presence or take your Holy Spirit from me.
Restore to me the joy of your salvation and grant
me a willing spirit, to sustain me.

Psalm 51:10-12

Chapter 6

Recovery

"*Golf puts a man's character on the anvil and his richest qualities —patience, poise, restraint— to the flame.*"

— Billy Casper

"Faith has its share of bunkers, and golf has its share of prayers."
— Max Lucado

Costantino Rocca of Italy was playing the final round of the 1995 British Open. On the eighteenth hole he was just two shots away from tying the leader, John Daly, and sending the round into extra holes. He was a short chip and putt away from accomplishing this feat, when he missed his chip shot, leaving the ball just off of the green. That chip shot could only be described as a disaster. Composing himself, he stepped up to the ball just off the green and sunk a very difficult thirty-footer to tie the match.

What a recovery!

The most important skill any golfer can acquire is the ability to recover from a bad situation. Whether it is recovering from a faulty shot, a poorly played hole, a terrible front nine, or yesterday's disaster round, every golfer faces such "recovery situations" sometime in his golfing season.

One of the fascinations of watching professional golf is seeing the pros recover from an errant shot, or surge after a double bogey to earn back those strokes with a string of birdies. The average golfer can identify with the problems the professionals get into occasionally. Seeing them recover and rise above their situations is part of the excitement of tournament play.

The problem most golfers have with recovering is attempting to make an impossible shot for the recovery and ending up in a worse situation.

Trying to make it to the green instead of laying up safely out of a bad lie can, more often than not, make the shot even more disastrous. Often golfers try to salvage strokes by taking more difficult shots to recover. These attempted recoveries are likely to end up errant themselves, adding to the problem.

The best way to recover is by relying on "a shot you know is in your bag." If it means laying up short of the green instead of going for it, that's what should be done. If it means using a short low punch shot to get out of the trees instead of going over the top to the green, that is the better percentage shot.

The most important point is to always *think recovery!* The rule is: "Don't give up; keep your mind and focus on the game." Neither anger nor frustration serves any useful purpose in a recovery situation.

"If you call on God to improve the results of a shot while it is still in motion, you are using 'an outside agency' and subject to appropriate penalties under the rules of golf."

— Henry Longhurst

⛳ REFLECTIONS

You may encounter difficult situations, make careless mistakes, or experience personal failure in your spiritual life. But the benefits of those experiences are only found in the recovery.

Be careful to keep your mind and heart in the game. Refuse to give up. The next shot could be the one to put you over the top. Always *think recovery!*

Remember the rule: "Play the shot you know is in your bag!"

The promises God has given us through faith in Him are there for your recovery. When faced with an impossible situation, your trust in God is the best recovery shot of all.

PRAYER

Lord, when I make mistakes, help me to recover. Help me never to give up, but to keep my mind in the game.

Help me to realize that when I recover, I am always better and smarter for it. Forgive me, strengthen me, and, by faith, encourage me to make the right recovery decisions.

Lord, I trust You in every situation. There is no better source of power and love to bring the recoveries I need than You.

SCRIPTURE

And we know that in all things God works for the good of those who love him, who have been called according to his purpose.

Romans 8:28

"I never pray on the golf course. Actually, the Lord answers my prayers everywhere except on the course."

— Rev. Billy Graham

"There are two things you can do with your head down — play golf and pray."
— Lee Trevino

Hazards are an integral part of the game of golf. Every golfer is aware that they are there, usually knowing the exact distance to them, and carefully planning every shot in order to avoid them.

All great players avoid hazards. Yet they also practice them, because they know that they can be encountered during any round. When it comes time to make a difficult hazard shot, such players are prepared in advance.

Hazards can be treacherous little spots in the lush manicured courses of towering trees and beautiful fairways. They can be watery or full of sand. They can be deep bunkers of grass which put the ball below the feet, or steep berms with the ball sitting up above the knees.

The purpose of hazards seems to be the total annihilation of a golfer's confidence and the complete destruction of his score.

Hazards call attention to a player's abilities, as well as his weaknesses.

They are the defining moments that can cause a golfer to look back at the end of a round and realize that he rose to the occasion or that he struggled desperately to "come out" with some vestige of his dignity intact.

But hazards also make the character of any course. They are the bitter or sweet spice in the experience of an otherwise uneventful round of golf.

Who can't appreciate the clear blue color of water surrounding a green, or the bright clean appearance of sparkling white sand encircling a dark smooth putting surface?

Most of the signature holes of famous golf courses around the world feature beautiful and memorable hazards. They are as much a part of the course as the lush fairways and verdant greens. Serious golfers learn, if not to enjoy hazards, at least to make the most of them.

"You are a fortunate person, indeed, if you can begin each day accepting the fact that during that day there will be ups and downs, good breaks and bad ones, disappointments, surprises, unexpected turns of events. At the same time wise golfers have learned to accept those adverse conditions on the golf course as representative of real life challenges."

— Roy Benjamin

REFLECTIONS

In your walk with God, you face many hazards. They can be so intimidating that if you aren't prepared, you can feel overwhelmed by their very existence and appearance.

Avoidance is always the best course to follow when confronting the hazards of life which can so easily discourage you. But, you must also consider the character, dimension, and maturity that hazards can bring into your life.

When you do encounter hazards or face bad situations, you must remember that God is able to provide a way out. He is not going to forget you or leave you there in a "trap."

Although some hazards are unavoidable, you can prepare for them by exercising your faith and trust in

God. You can recall the times God has been there for you, and have confidence that He will never leave you alone nor forsake you in your time of need.

🏌 Prayer

Lord, help me to be aware of the hazards in life's course, to judge the distance to them, and to avoid those things that can so easily trip me up.

Prepare me for the hazards I will face today. If I fall into a trap, pick me up. Show me the way out of every hard and discouraging situation.

Most importantly, teach me to use the faith and confidence Your promises have given me to overcome each challenge in life.

Lord, I cannot deny that there are hazards ahead. I see them all along the way toward the goal You have set for me. But I am not afraid, because I know that You are with me and will see me through to complete the course that is laid out before me.

⛳ SCRIPTURE

But remember this — the wrong desires that come
into your life aren't anything new and different.
Many others have faced exactly the same problems
before you. And no temptation is irresistible. You
can trust God to keep the temptation from being so
strong that you can't stand up against it, for he has
promised this and will do what he says. He will
show you how to escape temptation's power so that
you can bear up patiently against it.

1 Corinthians 10:13 TLB

Chapter 8

Good Equipment

"For most golfers the only difference between a one-dollar ball and a three-dollar ball is two dollars."

— Henry Beard

Mulligan's Laws

"It's a marriage. If I had to choose between my wife and my putter — I'd miss her."

— Gary Player

One of the best examples of the changes in golf equipment can be found in the golf ball.

The first golf balls were known as "featheries" because they had cores of feathers. They were made by taking "as many feathers as will fill a hat" and stuffing them tightly into a small round pouch made of leather or horsehide, which was then soaked in alum. As can be imagined, featheries didn't play very well in wet weather.

The 1840's saw the first golf balls made of gutta percha. This dried gum from the sapodilla tree could be melted and formed like wax, but cooled and hardened like plastic. Most importantly, the new golf balls made from this substance could also be mass produced.

In 1899 the Goodrich company introduced the first rubber-cored golf ball. It boasted the "Agrippa" pattern of raised pimples (called brambles).

In 1905 the Spaulding company introduced the first rubber-cored ball that was truly white. Previously golf balls had been painted white. Spaulding's ball was made of naturally white balata which was softer than gutta percha, and less likely to cut or nick.

In 1906 the pimples were changed to "dimples" by William Taylor. In 1930 the optimum dimple was determined to be between 0.012 inch and 0.0125 inch on a 1.62-inch ball. This is the standard today.

The maximum velocity allowed by the United States Golf Association is 250 feet per second. Any ball testing higher is declared by the USGA to be unfair, unsafe, and illegal.

Today golf equipment is big business. New club designs have cavity weighting, perimeter weighting, stiff or flexible shafts, graphite or steel (even "bubble") shafts, jumbo heads, titanium heads — and the list goes on and on.

Big equipment manufacturers are associated with outstanding professional golfers. Every serious amateur is looking for that extra edge in equipment that will help shave strokes off his game.

Each new technological announcement excites golfers looking for that instant improvement in performance. Everyone is looking for the new club that will add distance or accuracy to his shots, that "better" ball that will go farther and spin better.

But it is important to remember that new equipment should always be sized according to one's body and game. It has been shown that golfers definitely benefit from equipment that is properly "fitted" in this way.

Properly fitting equipment will allow a golfer to swing naturally and easily, which will enhance individual results on the course.

"One of the advantages bowling has over golf is that you seldom lose a bowling ball."

— Don Carter

REFLECTIONS

Most of us have learned by experience that there are few things more difficult than trying to accomplish something on the golf course with equipment that is just not suited to us individually.

In the same way, we have difficulty when we find ourselves trying to live a mass-produced spiritual life. Often the problem is that we are going through spiritual exercises that are lacking in uniqueness and individuality. We model ourselves after others and then wonder why we are not as satisfied and successful as they seem to be.

The reason you cannot blindly imitate others is because God has a plan and purpose that is uniquely yours. He knows exactly what fits you. He has something so specific and wonderful for you to accomplish that He will equip you with everything you need to fulfill the individual dream and goal He has in mind.

You must not look at other people's abilities and gifts to decide what God has for you. He has personally and purposefully custom fitted the equipment you need to serve Him as only you can.

⛳ Prayer

Lord, fit me with the abilities and gifts that You know are just right for me. Then teach me to make maximum use of what You have given me.

I know that only the equipment You have specifically provided me as an individual will be the most effective in my life.

Thank You for a relationship so personal and so unique that it is different from that of any other person on earth.

⛳ Scripture

May the God of peace....equip you with everything good for doing his will, and may he work in us what is pleasing to him, through Jesus Christ, to whom be glory for ever and ever. Amen.

Hebrews 13:20,21

Chapter 9

"Ben Hogan didn't have the prettiest swing in the world, but Ben Hogan knew his game better than anyone else knew theirs."

— Harvey Penick

"Golf is the hardest game in the world. There's no way you can ever get it. Just when you think you do, the game jumps up and puts you into your place."

— Ben Crenshaw, 1995
Masters Champion

How much confidence can anyone have in every club that he puts in his hand? Does any golfer know for sure exactly what a particular club will do with his swing?

How well a player knows every element of his game determines how much control he will have over every round of golf he plays.

Club distance is one of the basics involved in "knowing your game." Exactly how far the ball will travel with each club is a key element of golf which must be mastered.

Distance is so important to the golfer that everything from the tee box, the shrubs, and the sprinkler heads tell him how far away he is from the center of the green. Courses provide guide books to each hole and its various landmarks to help players judge distances.

But all the help in the world is to no avail if the individual player doesn't know his own club distances. The best golfers know their clubs and just what they can do with each one of them.

For the beginner, one of the most frustrating aspects of golf is the fact that he hits a nine-iron shot just as far as a five-iron shot. He is never really sure just how far each shot will travel. Poorly played shots give the inexperienced player a distorted picture of what each club is designed to accomplish.

Practice will help him learn the correct distances of each club — which is very important to good golf.

Making good decisions based upon a personal knowledge of "your own game" is part of the joy and fun of playing golf.

Knowledge of the various conditions encountered and how to overcome adversity raises the game to another level.

The confidence a player feels as he stands over a putt, knowing just the right speed and line, is truly inspiring. The understanding that he can pick the ball out of the sand and land it softly on the green just where he wants it is satisfying. There is nothing in the world of golf to compare with the sense of security that comes with knowing that whatever the distance to the pin, "This club will get me there."

Golf has always been a game of skill, with just the right mix of luck to make it exciting. But, with time and experience, there comes a day when the balancing scales seem to tip, and the golfer knows he has crossed over to a place where skill has taken the upper hand. At that moment, he has taken control of the game and doesn't want to give it up. It is both exciting and rewarding. At that moment, he is beginning to "know his game."

REFLECTIONS

Maturity in your spiritual life is a lot like "knowing your game." The level of confidence you experience in your faith comes from a "knowing" deep in your heart.

You know exactly where you stand in your relationship with God by His grace and the assuring presence of the Holy Spirit.

As you face challenges, God reveals to you "the distance" in each situation you face.

You step up, knowing by faith that God's work in your life will get you where you need to be.

Your life begins to focus on the purpose and calling of God. The balancing scales seem to tip the other way from luck or chance toward faith and confidence in His plan and purpose for you.

The instant you know that you have made Jesus Christ the Lord of your life is the defining moment you truly begin to "know your game."

PRAYER

Lord, give me the control and confidence I need to trust You in every situation. Help me to properly measure the distance in each of the challenges I face.

The more I know about who I am, the more I marvel at Your power to change me.

The deep sense of knowing who I am and what You have done for me gives purpose and direction.

SCRIPTURE

This is the confidence we have in approaching God:
that if we ask anything according to his will, he
hears us. And if we know that he hears us —
whatever we ask — we know that we have
what we asked of him.

1 John 5:14,15

"It is nothing new or original to say that golf is played one stroke at a time. But it took me many years to realize it."

— Bobby Jones

"You have to make corrections in your game a little bit at a time. It's like taking your medicine. A few aspirins will probably cure what ails you, but the whole bottle might just kill you."

— Harvey Penick

Golf's greatest champions have many unique strengths and qualities which set them apart from their peers. They bring something extra to the game that goes beyond the stroke and power in the mechanics of the golf swing. They have an absolute command of concentration and focus. They have the ability to analyze a situation and know when to play the percentages and when to gamble. They have the judgment and self-discipline to make the most of good situations and the best of bad situations.

They have control of their nerves and emotions under severe pressure, which enables them to maintain their rhythm and timing. But, above all else, they have the ambition to win.

Concentration and control are the basis for "managing your game."

How well a player focuses and retains composure in the face of adversity will determine the degree of management he will experience in his game.

"Course management" has to do with selecting the exact shots to be played during a certain round on a specific course.

"Managing your game" refers to the personal control over self that is exercised throughout that particular round. It involves the maintenance of the positive thoughts and courage necessary to make the best judgments about the game. Lapses in concentration or judgment, along with the fear of failure, will influence shot selection as well as shot making.

When playing with other people, you will find yourself playing their game and not your own. Some golfers make so many adjustments and changes that they never really know what their game is all about.

"Managing your game" is about knowing what you can do and what you cannot do, and applying that knowledge throughout the round in various situations by concentrating on strengths and avoiding weaknesses.

"The best stroked putt in a lifetime does not bring the aesthetic satisfaction of a perfectly hit wood or iron shot. There is nothing to match the whoosh and soar, the almost magical flight of a beautifully hit drive or a 5-iron."

— Al Barkow

REFLECTIONS

Just as in the game of golf, you can use the same qualities of "managing your game" in your spiritual life.

You may know what you should do, you may even know how to do it, but you may lack direction and purpose in your decision making. Poor choices can often lead to failure.

It is precisely in the "management of your game" that God wants to step into your life.

God wants to be there to give comfort for your nerves and control of your emotions so that you are able to face life's difficulties with faith and courage.

Just as golf must be played one stroke at a time, so life must be lived one day at a time. The key to happiness and success is trusting God to provide the focus and self-discipline you need to face each moment with the assurance and confidence that He is in control.

PRAYER

Lord, help me to manage my life through Your power, love, and grace. Help me to make the decisions that will cause me to become the most effective person I can be.

I realize that the more I turn my life over to Your management, the closer I come to enjoying everything You have planned for me.

Management of my life is a spiritual decision, one that will guide me through every situation I may face. So, I give myself to You and affirm Your control of my life.

Help me not to try to play someone else's game, but to depend on You for the self-control and wisdom I need to live a happy and successful life.

Today I surrender my life to Your plan, purpose, and management.

SCRIPTURE

Commit to the LORD whatever you do, and your
plans will succeed.

Proverbs 16:3

Chapter 11

The Mental Game

"I say this without any reservation whatsoever: It is impossible to outplay an opponent you can't outthink."

— Lawson Little

"Thinking must be the hardest thing to do in golf, because we do so little of it."

— Harvey Penick

The game of golf requires a unique set of physical skills which come from hours of practice and development. The application of those skills throughout a round of golf involves thinking and analytical decision making which few golfers master.

To some, golf is a game of escape. They don't want to think about anything. The course is a place to get away from it all. For these people, golf is an excuse to spend hours with friends in a beautiful outdoor environment.

Their only interest is camaraderie, unencumbered by office politics, social status, or peer pressure.

There doesn't seem to be anything terribly wrong about this approach to the game. But people miss so much of the enjoyment of the game when they set aside their thinking during the few hours they play a round.

There are both physical and mental elements to the game of golf.

Humans are physical beings with bodies that need exercise in order to feel good. Golf is great physical activity which can be enjoyed from youth through old age. It is a sport that can be continued long after youthful accomplishments are only memories.

But, there is also a mental aspect to life. It is this mental activity which helps us record and learn from our experiences. People actually feel better when they are using and exercising this part of their lives as well. The mental requirements of golf actually complement the physical side.

Thinking about what you are doing as you play a round of golf exercises the mental area of your life. Keeping your mind on the round as you make judgments and adjustments to your game helps you learn and improve. Improved thinking skills on the golf course are often the difference between a good player and a great player.

REFLECTIONS

Just as the mental game is important in golf, so thinking is also an important part of our spiritual lives. It is sad to realize how often we unconsciously allow ourselves to fall into the trap of using our faith as an escape from thinking.

God works in our lives through a renewing or changing of our minds.

It is the active mind which learns, receives new ideas, and adjusts to adverse circumstances whenever necessary. The use of our mental gifts and capabilities will help keep us in touch with what God is doing and saying to us.

In our daily existence we should be mentally active, as well as spiritually alert. Thinking about and learning how God is working in our lives will always improve our effectiveness.

PRAYER

Lord, teach me the mental aspects of my spiritual life. My relationship with You is not an escape from thinking, so help me to clearly understand what You are doing in my life.

Renew my mind, teaching me to be all You want me to be. I realize that I cannot serve You if my mind is not active and alert to what You are saying to me in every situation I encounter in my daily life.

SCRIPTURE

If any of you lacks wisdom, he should ask God, who gives generously to all without finding fault, and it will be given to him.

James 1:5

Chapter 12

Sportsmanship

"At holing you are to play your ball honestly for the hole, and not play upon your adversary's ball, not lying in your way to the hole."
— Rule Seven,
   Royal and Ancient Golf Club
   St. Andrews, Scotland

"Baseball reveals character; golf exposes it."
— Ernie Banks

Perhaps it is golf's beginnings as a sport of royalty which so deeply weaves sportsmanship throughout the fabric of its rules and play. Who would dare cheat the king or be discourteous to royalty? Strict adherence to rules and a total sense of sportsmanship would be the only way to engage in a sport against such powerful opponents.

Throughout its long and illustrious history, sportsmanship has always been the essence of golf. No one exemplified this trait more than Bobby Jones.

In the 1925 U.S. Open, Jones' ball moved when he addressed it. No one saw it move, so Jones called the penalty on himself.

That penalty ended up costing him the championship. When asked about it later, Jones replied, "There's only one way to play the game...."

When he was applauded for his honesty and integrity, Jones was appalled, saying that to applaud a player for not cheating was like applauding someone for not robbing a bank.

Learning techniques of hitting the ball, putting, and judging distances may give you the ability to *master* the game. But, Bobby Jones was right when he said there is only one way to *play* the game.

Sportsmanship is the element which goes beyond the mechanics of *mastering* the game and into the love of *playing* the game.

Sportsmanship is a combination of course etiquette and the inherent fairness exemplified by the rules.

It is an attitude within one's self which says, "I'm going to do this right; any other way just isn't worth it, to myself or anyone I am playing with."

Cheating doesn't prove anything to your opponents or to yourself.

Sportsmanship means that the value of success resides within the fairness by which it is achieved.

"Golf, in fact, is the only game in the world in which a precise knowledge of the rules can earn one a reputation for bad sportsmanship."

— Patrick Campbell, golf instructor

⚲ REFLECTIONS

Sportsmanship in the game of golf is similar to love in the game of life.

You may master all of the mechanics of being a good person. You may go to church, read your Bible, pray regularly, give to the poor, maybe even share your faith with other people. These things are all wonderful and commendable.

But there is something more which takes your faith beyond the realm of purely religious activities and into the realm of a love-motivated existence.

Love is that important element which is a reflection of the very nature of God. It elevates what you *do* to the realm of what God *is* in your life.

Love adds music to the mechanics of spiritual activity. For anyone who wants to experience life as God planned it, loving others even when no one is looking is the "only way to play the game...."

PRAYER

Lord, help me to remember that playing without true sportsmanship is only cheating myself. Serving You without love is merely going through the motions.

May Your love motivate, strengthen, and encourage everyone with whom I share it.

Lord, help me to honor others and always do the right thing. Keep me mindful that fairness, honesty, and integrity are always the right play, even if no one is watching. Help me realize that it is not success but truth that will set me free and keep me free.

⛳ Scripture

Make every effort to add to your faith goodness;
and to goodness, knowledge; and to knowledge,
self-control; and to self-control, perseverance; and to
perseverance, godliness; and to godliness, brotherly
kindness; and to brotherly kindness, love. For if you
possess these qualities in increasing measure, they
will keep you from being ineffective and
unproductive in your knowledge of our
Lord Jesus Christ.

2 Peter 1:5-8

Chapter 13

"The sum total of the rules [of etiquette in golf], is thoughtfulness."

— Abe Mitchell

British Champion

"After the tee shots, the player whose ball lies farther from the hole plays first."

— USGA Rule #12

The rules of golf are a reflection of the etiquette and fairness which are an integral part of the entire game.

Golf has been called the most "civilized" of sports. The player with the lowest score on the previous hole receives "honors" at the next tee. On the fairway, the "disadvantaged" player whose ball lies farthest from the hole shoots first. Likewise, on the green, the "unfortunate" longest putt precedes the others. Much of the ambiance of the game is built into these concepts of courtesy, fairness, and honor.

Good players are totally aware of their fellow golfers' game in progress. They have the sensitivity to make gracious and courteous decisions seem comfortable and natural. They observe all the little amenities throughout the round, like not casting shadows on the green or walking in another player's line. They practice the subtle courtesies which reflect an appreciation of others.

Poor players are either totally unaware of or completely unconcerned with anyone else's circumstances. They plow their way through each round leaving unrepaired divots and moonscaped sand traps, offending everyone who happens to get in their way.

There are not many sports other than golf in which participants can be so competitive and yet so conscientious of sportsmanship and fair play. The rules themselves seem to say to the golfer, "Yes, you are competing, but you must also be courteous and fair."

"No one knows why the warning shout of 'Fore!' is used all over the world, but we do know the first person to shout it was a caddie named Herd, in 1854. One speculation is that it's a shortened version of 'Beware before!' — which is shouted by the British army artillery as a warning to the infantry in front of them. The infantry would lie down to let the cannonballs pass over their heads. Golfers are thus warned by fellow players that ducking might be a good idea."

— Armand Eisen

Golf: Life on the Course

REFLECTIONS

Like the game of golf, the game of life is an enigma. We are a part of a dysfunctional world with its hatred, self-centeredness, and sin; yet we are expected to follow a life of love for our neighbor and service to others.

In the Bible, Jesus has told us that whoever among us would be greatest must be the servant of all the others.

Just as the rules of golf express the concepts of fairness and courtesy, the attitudes of God are expressed in the commandments of Jesus when He said, "Love God with all your heart, and love your neighbor as yourself."

PRAYER

Lord, give me an awareness of where others may be in their spiritual progress.

Help me not to cast a shadow over their goals and aspirations. Let me give honor when honor is due and advantage to others when it will help them.

Help me to be fair in all my relationships and to encourage everyone who is playing with me to appreciate Your goodness and kindness.

SCRIPTURE

Finally, all of you, live in harmony with one another; be sympathetic, love as brothers, be compassionate and humble. Do not repay evil with evil or insult with insult, but with blessing, because to this you were called so that you may inherit a blessing.

1 Peter 3:8,9

Chapter 14

A Sense of History

"Golf was invented a billion years

ago — don't you remember?"

— Old Scottish Golf Saying

"If you are going to be a player people will remember, you have to win the open at St. Andrews."

— Jack Nicklaus

Golf, like most sports, is imbued with a tremendous sense of history. Great players, great courses, great tournaments all make up the five hundred plus years of history associated with the game.

The game of golf, as it is known today, is generally believed to have developed in Scotland. The first written record of golf appeared in 1457 during the reign of King James II.

The first golf club organization was formed in 1744 in Leith. It was called the Honorable Company of Edinburgh Golfers.

In 1754 the St. Andrews Society of Golfers was organized (later it became the Royal and Ancient Golf Club of St. Andrews). Originally the St. Andrews course was twenty holes. In 1764 some holes were combined to create eighteen more difficult holes. This became the standard from that point forward.

From its royal beginnings with kings and queens, throughout world wars, famines, plagues, governmental changes, technological advances (including Alan Shepard's 6-iron shot from the surface of the moon on Apollo 14, which he said "went for miles and miles"), golf has been a part of mankind's sports history as well as its social history.

Golf's recent explosion of popularity has spawned a flood of new products, technology, training methods, equipment, courses, and millions of new followers who are devoted to the game. This surge of interest has intensified the search for the latest and greatest new idea "guaranteed to make any player the envy of the course."

But nothing with such a great history will give up its secrets so easily. There is no magic instrument which will conquer the challenges of this most difficult of games. So far, nothing "new and improved" has been able to reveal any weakness in the shroud of difficulty protecting the simple idea of hitting a little white ball with a stick until it comes to rest in a small hole in the ground.

All of today's instructional videos and high-tech approaches to the game seem somehow to diminish the historical perspectives of it. Yet, despite all of the current changes and improvements, golf is still a game with a great sense of history.

The major tournaments focus attention every year on the great courses in the United States, Britain, and around the world.

Trophies held high above the head of this year's winner are engraved with the legends of the past, silent reminders that while everything seems to change, there is a continuity that the sport of golf brings to its loyal fans.

Year after year golf produces a new champion who captures and holds forever a place on the silver cup passed down through decades, even centuries, never to be forgotten.

Occasionally it may occur to a golfer that people have played this game for hundreds of years. There have always been birdies and eagles, bogeys and double bogeys, great putts and long drives on the same courses he too enjoys.

It may even strike the player as peculiar to realize that kings and queens have enjoyed this sport. Rich and poor alike have experienced our same frustrations, as well as the pure joy of a few hours of what Arnold Palmer once called "without a doubt the greatest game mankind has ever invented."

REFLECTIONS

We also have a great sense of heritage and history in our faith. The spiritual lives of great men and women of God have literally changed the world.

For centuries, prominent people of faith have impacted mankind with God's love and power. Their achievements and commitment are a testimony of God's mercy and grace.

In today's high-tech world of electronic churches and video spiritually, we can easily miss the simple message of reconciliation to God through Jesus Christ. This message has been an historical focal point of mankind from the beginning of time.

Generations of princes and paupers alike have experienced this simple truth that "God so loved the world, that He gave His only begotten Son, that whosoever believes in Him, should not perish but have everlasting life."

The lessons from our spiritual heritage are that God is faithful, His love endures forever, and the great things He has done through the ages He will continue to do in us.

PRAYER

Lord, thank You for the sense of heritage and history that is so much a part of my faith.

As I consider the things You have done in my life, I am reminded of how faithful You are. When I recall all that You have done for me, I have confidence for what lies ahead.

I realize that I am not alone in my struggles or in my triumphs, because there are others who have shared in this journey with me.

And, Lord, if there is a past of failures and mistakes, I know there is also a future of hope and faith.

Today, help me to start building a new sense of history for tomorrow.

⛳ SCRIPTURE

For everything that was written in the past
was written to teach us, so that through
endurance and the encouragement of the
Scriptures we might have hope.

Romans 15:4

Chapter 15

"What other people may find in poetry, I find in the flight of a good drive."

— Arnold Palmer

"I never exaggerate. I just remember big."
— Chi Chi Rodriquez

Golf fans the world over will long remember watching Ben Crenshaw sink the final putt on the eighteenth hole of the Augusta National Golf Club to win the 1995 Masters Tournament.

As he dropped his putter and bent at the waist with his face in his hands, overcome with the emotion of the moment, those who watched could feel at least some of that emotion with him.

The special moment experienced in the seconds following that historic putt sums up for many golfers the feelings accompanying any great moment in golf.

Whether you are a seasoned professional or a weekend amateur, there are times when golf seems to "let you have one," just so you will come back. Sometimes it is the last twenty-footer on the eighteenth green at the very end of a particularly terrible round. Or it may be the chip shot that goes in right after you have missed the two previous shots.

Golf is a game of great moments. The excitement of making a great shot or a long putt can turn the tide of emotions from total despair to pure joy — that moment when the mind says, "YES!" Often a spontaneous shout of joy accompanies a euphoric feeling of tremendous accomplishment.

Sportsmen who really love the game of golf realize that there are days on the course when everything comes together during a round. Each element and aspect of the game just seems to work. Every tee shot goes a little farther and straighter, every iron shot seems to click off the club face, every putt is made with that special confidence that comes from knowing exactly what to do and how to do it.

It is these moments that make for memories. They are the source of endless stories with friends who share a love of the game. These moments are the confidence boosts needed when faced with difficult circumstances. They recall success whenever failure seems to be the only alternative.

Difficulties seem less formidable after having experienced even a few victories.

"Golf is a game of days, and I can beat anyone on my day."

—Fuzzy Zoeller

REFLECTIONS

You will also experience, or have experienced, great moments in your spiritual life — times when your faith seems particularly strong.

These experiences in your relationship with God are defining moments. They make you feel close to God. You sense that something supernatural has happened and that, as a result, you will never be the same.

These times of refreshing and closeness to God are to be cherished.

Perhaps you remember your first prayer, or a special time alone with God.

Whatever it may be, these are turning points in your spiritual life, special moments to be remembered and cherished as long as you live.

🏌 PRAYER

Lord, it's the great moments I remember — times when I didn't think it was possible, but You were there.

Help me to remember the great moments of my spiritual life.

Thank You for always being dependable. Special times serve to remind me of Your involvement in my life.

🏌 SCRIPTURE

For you made me glad by your deeds, O, LORD; I
sing for joy at the works of your hands.

Psalms 92:4

Chapter 16

To Get Better, Just Play!

"I'm the best. I just haven't played yet."

— Muhammad Ali, on golf

"Golf is assuredly a mystifying game. It would seem that if a person has hit a golf ball correctly a thousand times, he should be able to duplicate the performance at will. But such is certainly not the case."

— Bobby Jones

The range is a place where golf shots are practiced. Golf shots are used to play the game of golf. But golf is much more than just a series of shots.

The point is, a golfer cannot play golf at the practice range. To really get better at the game, he must play the game!

Watching golf videos may help you understand something you are doing wrong. Imagining yourself on your favorite course may increase your desire to play. But imagination alone will not improve your game.

To get *better* at golf, a person has to *play* golf.

Many people play golf once or twice a year and can't figure out why they don't enjoy the game. Once-a-month golfers often lose interest because they don't see any improvement in their rounds. Some play so infrequently that they forget what they learned at a lesson or can't remember the basics from one round to the next.

Golf is learned by training muscles to remember and feel the way a club should swing. Playing golf exercises those trained muscles, just as the practice range does, but it also brings together all of the elements of the game.

When you play the game of golf, you go beyond just hitting the ball. You make many important decisions throughout the round, and you improve through the experience.

Consistently taking the time to play the game can be the difference between improving or just staying the same.

REFLECTIONS

We cannot imagine ourselves into a closer relationship with God.

We can't just talk about God and expect to experience any of the joy of serving Him.

We have to *do* it!

We can say that we have faith without really doing anything. But using our faith through the things that we accomplish with God is the only way to develop a closer relationship with Him.

We must not be content to just imagine ourselves as better. We must put godly principles into action in our life to see the results of real commitment and fulfillment.

PRAYER

Lord, help me to use the things You have taught me to bless other people.

I don't want to be an imaginary child of God. Help me to express my relationship with You in actions that will reflect Your grace and power.

Instead of just thinking about serving You, I want to do something with the gifts and abilities You have given me.

SCRIPTURE

Do not merely listen to the word, and so deceive yourselves. Do what it says. Anyone who listens to the word but does not do what it says is like a man who looks at his face in a mirror and, after looking at himself, goes away and immediately forgets what he looks like. But the man who looks intently into the perfect law that gives freedom, and continues to do this, not forgetting what he has heard, but doing it — he will be blessed in what he does.

James 1:22-25

Chapter 17

"It's nice to have people watching. They help me find my ball sometimes."

— Jack Nicklaus II

"Without the people, I'd be playing in front of trees for a couple of hundred dollars."

— Fuzzy Zoeller

Some people claim that watching golf on TV is about as exciting as watching grass grow. Yet, others videotape every major golf tournament televised.

To those who really love the game of golf, it is nearly as much fun to watch as it is to play.

Television moves from shot to shot, jumping around to the various holes where favorites are lining up putts or hitting those monster drives down the middle. The enjoyment of watching great players and exciting tournament finishes has made golf not only a favorite player sport, but a popular spectator sport as well.

Particularly enjoyable for many fans are the highlights on the evening news. For about sixty seconds viewers can watch four or five of the best shots of the day. With each shot they can say to themselves, "Wow, that was great!" — and quietly hope that within the next day or two they will be out getting the same results at the local course.

Watching golf events on television can be fun, but it is even better to attend a professional golf tournament. Walking the course with great players or just staying in one spot as various groups play through is a great experience.

There is something about the live scene that television cannot portray. The true layout of the course can be seen from a player's perspective, not just a quick flyover from a helicopter.

The greens are different, more dimensional than they appear on television. Tower shots are great for television cameras, but being there at eye level with the players is an unforgettable experience.

One special aspect of any professional event is the practice round days. The players are more relaxed. Some sign autographs and even chat with the gallery. Most are great sportsman and truly appreciate the fans who support the events.

Many golf enthusiasts are convinced that they feel more of a closeness to their favorite professionals than followers of any other sport.

Millions of fans may watch the professional quarterback throw the winning touchdown, or the big-league baseball player hit the monster home run, or the pro basketball player drive the lane for the spectacular slam dunk. But golf fans watching a professional sink a winning birdie putt can associate that shot with their own recent birdie or other success.

What is it that makes watching golf professionals so enjoyable? Many believe it is their consistency, control, and composure. They must be consistent in order to compete against other great players in a game in which just a few bad holes can ruin an entire round. They must always be in control of their shots, their game, and their circumstances. And they must maintain tremendous composure throughout the ups and downs of their round.

Watching golf professionals can also improve the viewer's game. Observing how the pros handle difficulties and opportunities can be a lesson to any aspiring golfer.

"At Augusta National in Georgia, the fabled home of the Masters Tournament, the captains of industry who make up the membership are actually forbidden — in writing — from shop talk of any kind on club grounds."

— Barbara Puett and Jim Apfelbaum

Golf Etiquette

REFLECTIONS

Just as we can benefit from the examples of golf professionals, we can also benefit from the examples of outstanding godly lives. Spiritual leaders, such as pastors or teachers, can provide the role models we desperately need today.

We can see first hand the great truths and principles working in the lives of other godly men and women.

Watching these people in a church setting is a lot like watching golf on TV. It is similar to seeing the course from a blimp. Church can be just as much a one- or two-dimensional experience as a televised golf tournament.

That's why we need the fellowship of other believers out in the real world. We need to walk with them through the entire course, watching their examples of consistency, control, and composure.

We should not ignore the godly men and women of principle we encounter. They are our examples. They inspire us. We see God working profoundly in their lives, and we know that He will help us as He has helped them.

PRAYER

Lord, thank You for the faithful friends and godly people You have brought into my life. Thank You for the example they are to me.

I am grateful that I can get a glimpse of You through their lives.

Lord, I know that I may be the example and encouragement someone else may need.

What a privilege it is to represent You. Help me to consistently be a reflection of Your grace, mercy, and love to others.

SCRIPTURE

Remember your leaders, who spoke the word of God to you. Consider the outcome of their way of life and imitate their faith. Jesus Christ is the same yesterday and today and forever.

Hebrews 13:7,8

"Golf has afforded me an opportunity permitted few men: to create on one of the broadest canvasses known to man and, in doing so, to complement and, sometimes, to improve on the work of the greatest Creator of all. Golf courses are built by men, but God provides the venues."

— Robert Trent Jones
World's leading golf
course architect

"While man's battle against himself is undoubtedly at the heart of golf's abiding appeal, the setting in which it is played is for most golfers, one of the most wonderful things about it."

— Herbert Warren Wind

The land which is today the Augusta National Golf Club was originally settled by a Belgian family in 1857 and was the location of the first nursery known in the South. The owner, Baron Prosper Jules Alphonse Berckmans, was a landscape architect, horticulturist, botanist, and artist.

Golfer Bobby Jones' first visit to the undeveloped 365 acres of land outside of Augusta, Georgia, was in December 1930. Later he wrote, "The experience was unforgettable. It seemed that this land had been lying here for years just waiting for someone to lay a golf course upon it."

Today Augusta National Golf Club is a national showcase of beauty and course design. The annual television broadcast of the Masters Tournament is as much a horticulturist's delight as it is an exciting tournament of championship professional golf.

The beautifully manicured deep green grasses make the stark white sand traps seem to glow. The azaleas provide rich colors that are so strong they seem to be deliberate natural distractions. The massive oak tree between the clubhouse and the second and seventh greens is more than two hundred years old. The wisteria vine at the corner of the clubhouse is said to be the oldest in the United States. Throughout the course and surrounding grounds there are markers identifying trees, flowering plants, and shrubs of historical significance.

This small piece of the world set aside and tended with such dedication and care is also one of the most difficult tests of a professional golfer's skills. This near perfect world of natural beauty seems so elegant and unspoiled, yet the world has seen it bring great champions to humility and despair.

Today lush green courses seem out of place in the arid beauty of the Southwestern United States. These desert courses are a stark contrast to the holes laid out beside the Pacific Ocean breakers at Pebble Beach, California. The tropical island courses among the lava flows of Hawaii are a world away from the sand dune grasses of the Old Course at St. Andrews, Scotland.

Great golf courses will always be judged by two criteria: how beautiful they are to view, and how challenging they are to play. From the towering trees and manicured fairways of the historical and famous courses, to the thousands of quaint and beautiful small town links throughout the world, golfers enjoy these settings which are created to be so appealing and yet so difficult.

"During World War II, the British dug wide trenches across the fairways of many of thier golf courses to keep German airplanes from using them as landing strips. Occasionally German bombers would sometimes attack golfers at play, a set of war rules was drawn up. One allowed that 'in competition during or while the bombs are falling, players may take cover without penalty for ceasing to play.' Good show. Not all the rules were as lenient, though. "A player whose stroke is affected by the simultaneous explosion of a bomb or shell, or by machine-gun fire, may play another ball from the same place. Penalty, one stroke."

— Robert Trent Jones, Ed.

Great Golf Stories

REFLECTIONS

The world is full of promises and possibilities as we experience the joy of a personal relationship with God.

But living a life of faith can be challenging. We should not get so caught up in the struggle of faith that we fail to see the beauty of the place where God has placed us.

He has blessed us richly.

Even though we may be facing the most difficult "shot" of our life, with our faith on the line, we can still step back, look around at all that God has blessed us with, and realize that we are in a place of magnificent beauty, prepared for us by God Himself.

PRAYER

Lord, when my path gets difficult, and the challenges seem more than I can bear, help me to see the beauty of where I am.

The joy of realizing how blessed I am is my encouragement.

Remind me that occasionally I need to step back, take a deep breath, perhaps just stop for a moment to realize where I am because of Your love for me.

The beauty I see on the golf course is a reminder of Your majesty and power. Help me to remember that the God Who created this venue is the same God Who created a new heart in me.

As I consider the beauty of my surroundings, may I come to understand even more how much You care for me.

⛳ SCRIPTURE

"Consider how the lilies grow. They do not labor or spin. Yet I tell you, not even Solomon in all his splendor was dressed like one of these. If that is how God clothes the grass of the field, which is here today, and tomorrow is thrown into the fire, how much more will he clothe you!"

Luke 12:27,28

"Golf is the only sport that a professional can enjoy playing with his friends. Can Larry Holmes enjoy fighting one of his friends?"

— Chi Chi Rodriquez

"Golf is like fishing and hunting. What counts is the companionship and fellowship of friends, not what you catch or shoot."

— George Archer

Friendships are one of the greatest benefits of golf. Some people play with the same group of friends every week. They wouldn't miss this time playing together for anything.

The time spent with friends on a golf course is one of the most enjoyable aspects of the sport.

Although most groups involve some type of competition during a round of golf, there is still the challenge of the course and the camaraderie of playing together and encouraging each other at each shot.

Handicaps equalize the play so that there can be challenges and competition for everyone. This helps two players with totally different capabilities compete in a friendly way.

Just about everyone has a favorite partner to play golf with. Together they make a team which has witnessed each other's best and worst days. Each may have played golf with lots of other people, but this one person is their best friend on the course.

Each knows exactly what the other is capable of shooting and what shot is totally beyond hope.

Each knows when to be quiet after a bad shot, and when to say just the right thing at just the right time.

Neither tries to rebuild a golf swing with unwanted advise, but does notice one or two little things that will help out the other.

If either could choose just one person to witness that once-in-a-lifetime hole in one, it would be the other person.

When the round is over, the two of them enjoy just relaxing for a few moments to relive the best shots of the round, or to talk about the "what-ifs." They understand how great the round could have been, as well as how good it really was.

At Christmas time or birthdays they always buy each other "golf things" — and appreciate it.

They may have one or two of each other's old clubs in their bag, just because they hit with it so well.

Sometimes such friendships last decades or even through great distances if one player moves away.

You are truly fortunate indeed to find one or two such great golfing friendships. You are most blessed if the friend is also your spouse.

Many husbands and wives enjoy the sport throughout their working lives and well into retirement. It is a great time to get away from the chores at home or the phone calls and disturbances of the office or work and share quality time together.

⚑ Reflections

Your friends and the love and fellowship you experience with them is important to your spiritual well being.

You need that special person or group of people with whom you can share your victories as well as your challenges. You find strength within these relationships.

You are truly blessed if you find the kindred heart of fellowship with another believer to share your journey of faith. What a blessing it is to have a friend who knows when to say something encouraging in the time of your greatest need, or just quietly be there because his or her presence is a strength to you.

How wonderful it is to have someone to share the good times as well as the "what-ifs" — someone to sit down with you when it is all over to reflect on how God moved in ways you may not have even noticed.

Treasure the friendships you have. They are more valuable than anything you possess.

🏌 PRAYER

Lord, thank You for the friends I have.

Help me to be the kind of friend other people need.

Help me to listen and encourage others when I can. As a friend, help me to lead others to You.

And most of all, I am thankful for Your friendship.

SCRIPTURE

"I no longer call you servants, because a servant does not know his master's business. Instead, I have called you friends, for everything that I learned from my Father I have made known to you. You did not choose me, but I chose you and appointed you to go and bear fruit — fruit that will last. Then the Father will give you whatever you ask in my name. This is my command: Love each other."

John 15:15-17

Additional copies of this book are available
at your local bookstore.

Tulsa, Oklahoma